PRESIDENTS' DAY

by Robin Nelson

first step nonfiction

Lerner Publications Company · Minneapolis

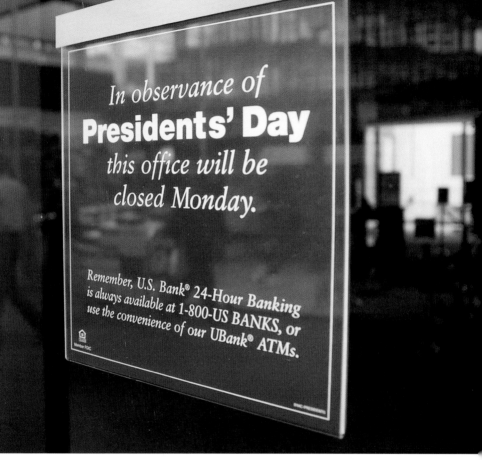

We **celebrate** Presidents' Day every year.

February

Sunday	Monday	Tuesday	Wednesday	Thursday	Friday	Saturday
					1	2
3	4	5	6	7	8	9
10	11	12	13	14	15	16
17	Presidents' Day 18	19	20	21	22	23
24	25	26	27	28		

This holiday is in February.

The **president** is the leader
of the United States.

This holiday began as a
way to **honor** two presidents.

George Washington was our first president.

George Washington fought
for our **freedom.**

Abraham Lincoln worked to keep our country together.

Abraham Lincoln helped
end **slavery.**

These presidents believed in freedom.

They believed in being fair.

The United States has had many great presidents.

Today we honor all our presidents on Presidents' Day.

We celebrate our leaders.

We celebrate our country.

On Presidents' Day, we learn about great presidents.

We practice being good
leaders.

Presidents' Day Timeline

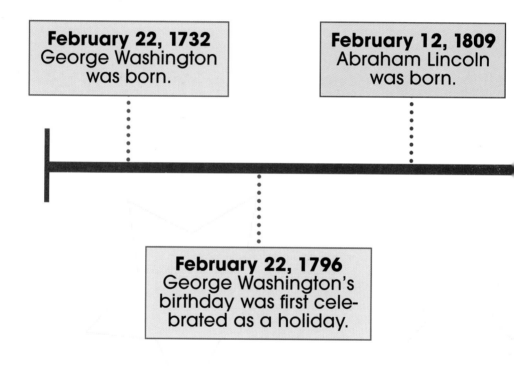

February 22, 1732
George Washington
was born.

February 12, 1809
Abraham Lincoln
was born.

February 22, 1796
George Washington's
birthday was first cele-
brated as a holiday.

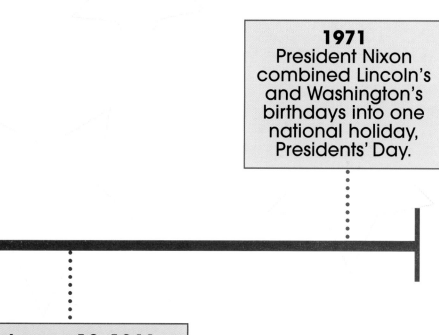

1971
President Nixon combined Lincoln's and Washington's birthdays into one national holiday, Presidents' Day.

February 12, 1866
Abraham Lincoln's birthday was first celebrated as a holiday.

Presidents' Day Facts

 George Washington is sometimes called the father of our country.

The Washington Monument in Washington, D.C., was built to honor George Washington. It stands 555 feet high. Millions of people visit it every year.

Abraham Lincoln had very little schooling. Lincoln taught himself how to read and write. He also taught himself math.

People trusted Abraham Lincoln and called him "Honest Abe."

Abraham Lincoln was assassinated on April 14, 1865, a few days after the Civil War ended. He was shot by John Wilkes Booth while attending a play with his wife. He died the next day.

The Lincoln Memorial in Washington, D.C., was built to honor Abraham Lincoln. It is a marble building containing a huge statue of Lincoln. Millions of people visit it each year.

Glossary

 celebrate – to have a party or special activity to honor a special occasion

 freedom – not being ruled by others

 honor – to show special respect for

 president – a leader of a country or group

 slavery – owning another person

Index

Photos reproduced with the permission of: Corbis Royalty Free, cover, pp. 17, 22 (second from top); © Todd Strand/Independent Picture Service, pp. 2, 3, 22 (top); © Ronald Reagan Library, p. 4; © Betty Crowell, pp. 5 (left), 20; © Diane Meyer, pp. 5 (right), 15, 21, 22 (middle); Library of Congress, pp. 6, 7; © North Wind Pictures, pp. 8, 9, 11, 22 (bottom); Library of Congress, p. 10; © Finley Holiday Films, p. 12; George Bush Presidential Library, pp. 13, 16; © AFP/ CORBIS, pp. 14, 22 (second from bottom).

This book is available in two editions:
Library binding by Lerner Publications Company, a division of Lerner Publishing Group, Inc.
Soft cover by LernerClassroom, a division of Lerner Publishing Group, Inc.
241 First Avenue North
Minneapolis, MN 55401 USA

For reading levels and more information, look up this title at www.lernerbooks.com.

Library of Congress Cataloging-in-Publication Data

Nelson, Robin, 1971–
        Presidents' Day / by Robin Nelson.
            p.   cm. — (First step nonfiction)
        Includes index.
        Summary: A simple introduction to why we celebrate Presidents' Day.
        ISBN 978–0–8225–1272–1 (lib. bdg. : alk. paper)
        ISBN 978–0–8225–1316–2 (pbk. : alk. paper)
        ISBN 978–0–8225–8005–8 (eBook)
        1. Presidents' Day—Juvenile literature. 2. Presidents—United States—History—Juvenile literature. [1. Presidents' Day.] I. Title. II. Series.
        E176.8.N45 2003
        394.261—dc21   2001007839

Manufactured in China
7 – SS – 1/1/14